JAZZ

Collection of Jazz Favorites for Young Voices

Arrangements by
Roger Emerson, Kirby Shaw, Mac Huff,
Steve Zegree and Tom Anderson

T0101680

Table of Contents

HAL•LEONARD® CORPORATION

7777 W. BLUEMOUND RD. P.O. BOX 13819 MILWAUKEE, WI 53213

Visit Hal Leonard Online at
www.halleonard.com

BASIN STREET BLUES

Arranged by
TOM ANDERSON

Words and Music by
SPENCER WILLIAMS

New Or - leans, ___ land of dreams, ___ you'll nev - er know how nice it seems or

just how much it real - ly means. ___ Glad to be; ___ yes, sir - ee, ___ where

wel - come's free, ___ dear to me, ___ where I can lose ___

my Ba - sin Street blues. ___

cresc.

4

CHOO CHOO CH' BOOGIE

Arranged by
ROGER EMERSON

Words and Music by VAUGHN HORTON,
DENVER DARLING and MILTON GABLER

Medium fast swing (♩ = 144)

Lyrics:

1. I'm head-in' for the sta-tion with my pack on my back, I'm
(2.) gon-na set-tle down be-side the rail-road track, and

tired of trans-por-ta-tion in the back of a hack. I love to hear the rhy-thm of the
live the life o' Ri-ley in a beat-en down shack. So when I hear the whis-tle I can

click - e - ty clack, and hear the lone - some whis - tle, see the smoke from the stack. And
peep through the crack, and watch the train a - roll - in' when it's ball - in' the jack.* For

Opt. harmony
cresc.

pal a - round with dem - o - crat - ic fel - lows named "Mac",} So take me right back to the
I just love the rhy - thm of the click - e - ty clack,}

cresc.

track, Jack! Choo choo,_____ choo choo ch' boo - gie. Woo

woo,_____ woo woo ch' boo - gie. Choo choo,_____ choo

* to move quickly; also a dance step

choo ch' boo-gie; take me right back to the track, Jack! I'm

2 track, Jack! Dwee____ 'n doo bah doo bah doo bah dwee doo daht. Dwee_

__ 'n doo bah doo bah doo bah dwee doo daht. Doot n' doot n' dwee ah.

Doo bah doo wah.__ Doot n' doot n' dwee ah. Doo bah doo wah.__

28 Optional: Repeat ms. 28-39 for scat solos

9

hear the lone-some whis-tle, see the smoke from the stack. And pal a-round with dem-o-crat-ic

fel-lows named "Mac", So take me right back to the track, Jack! Choo

choo,_____ choo choo ch' boo-gie. Woo woo,_____ woo

woo ch' boo-gie. Choo choo,_____ choo choo ch' boo-gie;

I'VE GOT THE WORLD ON A STRING

Arranged by
STEVE ZEGREE

Lyric by TED KOEHLER
Music by HAROLD ARLEN

JAVA JIVE

Arranged by
KIRBY SHAW

**Words and Music by
MILTON DRAKE and BEN OAKLAND**

21 Part I

slip me a slug___ from that won-der-ful mug___ and I'll cut a rug___ 'til I'm

Part II

Oo___ Oo___

C7 B7 C7

snug in a jug.___ A slice of on-ion and a raw one,___ *End opt. solo*

G

All *Opt. solo* 29

draw one,___ wait-er, wait-er, perc-o-la-tor! I love cof-fee, I love tea,___

C# D7 G B♭dim7 Am7sus Am7 D7

22

From The Pink Panther

THE PINK PANTHER

**Arranged by
ROGER EMERSON**

By HENRY MANCINI

Finger Snaps on 2 & 4 may be added throughout if desired.

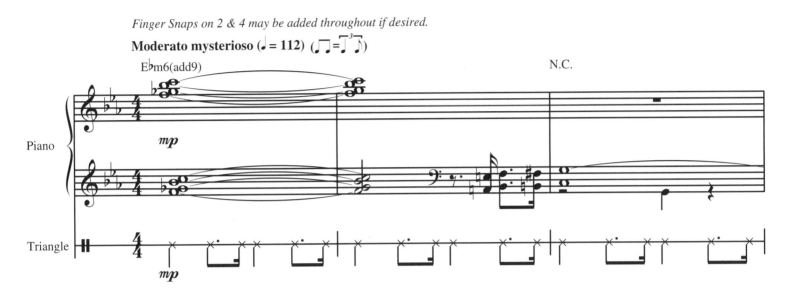

All voices sing Part II the first time; parts divide 2nd time.

Continue to m. 19

doo dn doo doo doo.

Doo dn doo doo doo.

21

Part I   *mf*

Doo doot   doo

Part II   *mf*

Doo dn doo doo doo.

Doo

mf

24

TUXEDO JUNCTION

Arranged by
MAC HUFF

Words by BUDDY FEYNE
Music by ERSKINE HAWKINS,
WILLIAM JOHNSON and JULIAN DASH

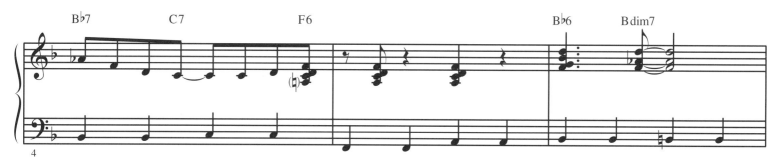

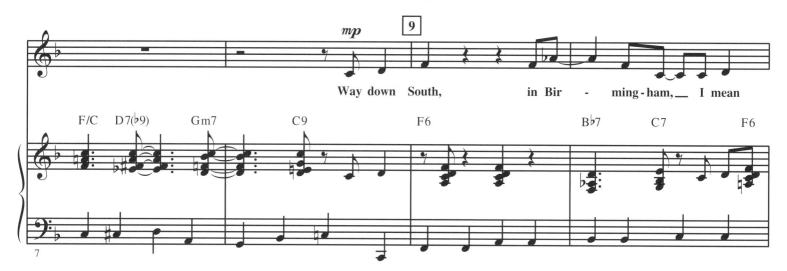